THIS

Habit Tracker & Goal Planner

BELONGS TO

_____

Habits vs. Goals

*"First forget inspiration.
Habit is more dependable.
Habit will sustain you whether you're inspired or not...
Habit is persistence in practice."*
— Octavia Butler

We all have goals, things that we want to achieve in our lives — getting into a better shape, running a marathon, writing a book, learning a new language, building a successful business, and so on.

What is the problem with goals?

To start with, goals require constant willpower to keep them in mind and direct our actions towards them.

Until you get there you can be in a constant state of underachievement.

And last but not least, achieving a goal can end with people reverting to their problematic states.
People lose the desired weight and erase their progress by getting back to overeating and not exercising. They win the desired amount of money only to fall in debt afterwards.

So how can we avoid these problems and achieve our goals at the same time?

The Benefits of Habits

You want to achieve your goals and keep growing instead of taking more steps back? Then you should stop thinking only in terms of goals and start developing a system of good habits that will take you where you want to be.

Good habits will help you reach your goals. Bad habits will hinder you. Start introducing the necessary good habits in your daily routine.

Let's say you want to lose weight.
Determine what habits will help you to achieve your goal, such as drinking water first thing in the morning and before each meal, taking a 20-minute walk every day, keeping a food journal, etc.
Those habits will have a much wider impact on your life than simply reaching your goal weight for a certain period of time. Habits can last for life.

Focus on developing good habits and once formed, your habits will operate automatically and take you step by step on a daily basis closer to your desired outcome.
And your dream life.

How Long to Form a New Habit?

You have probably heard more than once by more than one source this number: 21 days. This number sounds small enough and achievable but unfortunately if you really want to succeed you need to set your expectations straight.
May be if it comes to developing a bad habit even 3 repetitions will be enough but good habits take time. Most often much more than 21 days.

So how much time really does it actually take to form a new habit?

According to a recent study, daily habits like doing yoga for 10 minutes every morning, or drinking water before every meal, require at least 2 months for the new habit to become automatic.

66 days to be exact.

This number may be very different depending on the person and the circumstances. In any case do not get discouraged if you don't get it in quick 21 days. Embrace the slow walk to greatness and focus on your patience, persistence and daily repetitions.

Why Track Your Habits?

If you have ever tried to instill a new daily habit before, you know that this can be pretty challenging to maintain for the long term. This is where habit-tracking journals come in handy.

Here is why you should keep track of your habits:

- **Consistency** – Being consistent is of paramount importance when creating a new or breaking an old habit. Keeping a habit journal will make you check in on your habits on a daily basis.

- **Accountability** – In the absence of tracking, you will not have an accountability system in place to warn you when you miss a day.

- **Fulfillment** – Checking those habits regularly gives you a great sense of fulfillment every day.

- **Motivation** – It is that sense of fulfillment that will help you stay motivated. Plus, you really won't want to break a nice streak of consecutive days once you see it in your habit journal.

- **Eliminating bad habit triggers** – The key to eliminating a bad habit is to find its underlying triggers. A good habit tracking journal will help you track and deal with those triggers too.

- **Enjoying the process** – If you look at your habits with the mindset of just being consistent rather than being perfect a lot of the pressure is eliminated. You will be able to fully enjoy your progress.

Getting Your Dream Life As Easy As 1-2-3

1 Introduce your habits to your daily life but *be specific!* Soon is not a time. Some is not a number. Schedule your habits into your life by adding them to your calendar or tying them to a specific routine.

Want to be happier? Keep a small stone (or a coin, a paper clip, anything) in your pocket and tell yourself one thing you are grateful for every time you touch it. The stone will be the reminder.
Want to drink more water? Drink 2 glasses of water after waking up each day.

Same trigger, same sequence, same way, every day.
Being specific will give habits their own space in your life and help you stick to them automatically.

2 *Track your habits.* When setting new habits, we have a lot more resistance to deal with. Having a tracking system and accountability will help you stay committed to your new habits. Plus, tracking habits on a daily basis gives a sense of everyday accomplishment. This in turn will give you more motivation to stay on track.

3 No need to be perfect, you can *make mistakes*. You are human and small hiccups are perfectly fine. Skipping a day and making a mistake here and there will not make you a failure and will have no measurable impact on your long-term habits. Just move on and get back on track, that's the way to success.

FIRST WE MAKE OUR HABITS, AND THEN OUR HABITS MAKE US.

What habits are you making?

My **66-DAY JOURNEY** to

improve my life

starts here:

___ / ___ / ___

Plan for the next 66 days

Choose your goals. What do you want to achieve?

┌─ *Goal(s)* ─────────────────────────┐
│   │
│   │
│   │
│   │
└──────────────────────────────────────┘

Know your reasons. Why do you want this, why is it important to you?

┌─ *Why?* ────────────────────────────┐
│   │
│   │
│   │
│   │
│   │
│   │
│   │
└──────────────────────────────────────┘

*Think of habits that can help you achieve your goals.
They can be big or small, easy or hard. Remember to be
specific and schedule your habits into your daily routine
by writing down what should trigger the habit or when
you should take action.*

Habit	Trigger / Time

Week #1

What is your most important task for this week?

This week's focus

What I am grateful or excited about:

_____

_____

_____

_____

_____

What will make me happier this week:
/Small things that bring smiles matter!/

_____

_____

_____

_____

_____

Other notes:

_____

_____

_____

_____

_____

> "Don't make change too complicated,
> just begin."

My habits this week:	M	T	W	T	F	S	S

Did something go wrong & my response to it:

_____

_____

Something to make next week better:

_____

_____

How I feel about my habits this week:

Week #2

What is your most important task for this week?

This week's focus

What I am grateful or excited about:

_____
_____
_____
_____
_____

What will make me happier this week:
/Small things that bring smiles matter!/

_____
_____
_____
_____
_____

Other notes:

_____
_____
_____
_____

> "Habit is a cable; we weave a thread each day,
> and at last we cannot break it."

My habits this week:	M	T	W	T	F	S	S

Did something go wrong & my response to it:

_____

_____

Something to make next week better:

_____

_____

How I feel about my habits this week:

Week #3

What is your most important task for this week?

This week's focus

What I am grateful or excited about:

_____
_____
_____
_____
_____

What will make me happier this week:
/Small things that bring smiles matter!/

_____
_____
_____
_____
_____

Other notes:

_____
_____
_____
_____
_____

> "The secret of your success is found in your daily routine."

My habits this week:	M	T	W	T	F	S	S

Did something go wrong & my response to it:

_____

_____

Something to make next week better:

_____

_____

How I feel about my habits this week:

Week #4

What is your most important task for this week?

This week's focus

What I am grateful or excited about:

What will make me happier this week:
/Small things that bring smiles matter!/

Other notes:

"Motivation is what gets you started.
Habit is what keeps you going."

My habits this week:	M	T	W	T	F	S	S

Did something go wrong & my response to it:

_____

_____

Something to make next week better:

_____

_____

How I feel about my habits this week:

Week #5

What is your most important task for this week?

This week's focus

What I am grateful or excited about:

_____
_____
_____
_____
_____

What will make me happier this week:
/Small things that bring smiles matter!/

_____
_____
_____
_____
_____

Other notes:

_____
_____
_____
_____

"You must begin to think of yourself as becoming the person you want to be."

My habits this week:	M	T	W	T	F	S	S

Did something go wrong & my response to it:

_____

_____

Something to make next week better:

_____

_____

How I feel about my habits this week:

Week #6

What is your most important task for this week?

— This week's focus —

What I am grateful or excited about:

_____
_____
_____
_____
_____

What will make me happier this week:
/Small things that bring smiles matter!/

_____
_____
_____
_____
_____

Other notes:

_____
_____
_____
_____

> *"Perseverance is failing 19 times and succeeding the 20th."*

My habits this week:	M	T	W	T	F	S	S

Did something go wrong & my response to it:

_____

_____

Something to make next week better:

_____

_____

How I feel about my habits this week:

Week #7

What is your most important task for this week?

This week's focus

What I am grateful or excited about:

_____
_____
_____
_____
_____

What will make me happier this week:
/Small things that bring smiles matter!/

_____
_____
_____
_____
_____

Other notes:

_____
_____
_____
_____

My habits this week:	M	T	W	T	F	S	S

Did something go wrong & my response to it:

_____

_____

Something to make next week better:

_____

_____

How I feel about my habits this week:

☹ 🙁 😐 🙂 😊

Week #8

What is your most important task for this week?

┌───┐
│ *This week's focus* │
│ │
│ │
│ │
│ │
└───┘

What I am grateful or excited about:

_____
_____
_____
_____
_____

What will make me happier this week:
/Small things that bring smiles matter!/

_____
_____
_____
_____
_____

Other notes:

_____
_____
_____
_____
_____

> "Laziness is nothing more than the habit of
> resting before you get tired."

My habits this week:	M	T	W	T	F	S	S

Did something go wrong & my response to it:

_____

_____

Something to make next week better:

_____

_____

How I feel about my habits this week:

Week #9

What is your most important task for this week?

This week's focus

What I am grateful or excited about:

_____
_____
_____
_____
_____

What will make me happier this week:
/Small things that bring smiles matter!/

_____
_____
_____
_____
_____

Other notes:

_____
_____
_____
_____
_____

> "Everyday do something that will inch you closer to a better tomorrow."

My habits this week:	M	T	W	T	F	S	S

Did something go wrong & my response to it:

_____

_____

Something to make next week better:

_____

_____

How I feel about my habits this week:

Week #10 (last 3 days)

What is your most important task for this week?

This week's focus

What I am grateful or excited about:

_____
_____
_____
_____
_____

What will make me happier this week:
/Small things that bring smiles matter!/

_____
_____
_____
_____
_____

Other notes:

_____
_____
_____
_____

My habits:	3	2	1	

Did something go wrong & my response to it:

_____

_____

Something to make my future weeks better:

_____

_____

How I feel about my habits this week:

☹ 🙁 😐 🙂 😄

My 66-Day Habit Challenge
Reflection

How do I feel about each of my desired new habits?

Habit	*Result*

> "Learn from yesterday, live for today,
> hope for tomorrow."

How did I grow during this period?

_____
_____
_____
_____
_____
_____

How could I still improve?

_____
_____
_____
_____
_____
_____

Other thoughts:

_____
_____
_____
_____
_____
_____
_____
_____
_____
_____

Congratulations!
You completed the 66-day Habit Challenge!

"REMEMBER, YOU HAVE BEEN CRITICIZING YOURSELF FOR YEARS AND IT HASN'T WORKED. TRY APPROVING OF YOURSELF AND SEE WHAT HAPPENS."

MY MONTHLY

Habit Tracker & Goal Planner

Month #1

Choose your monthly goals and determine your habits:

Goal(s)

Habit | **Trigger / Time**

My Habits

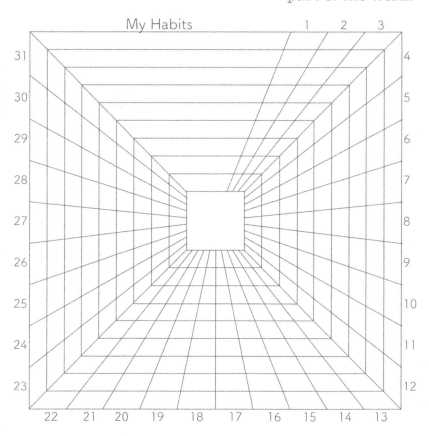

Did something go wrong & my response to it:

_____

_____

Something to make next month better:

_____

_____

How I feel about my habits this month:

Month #2

Choose your monthly goals and determine your habits:

--- Goal(s) ---

--- Habit --- --- Trigger / Time ---

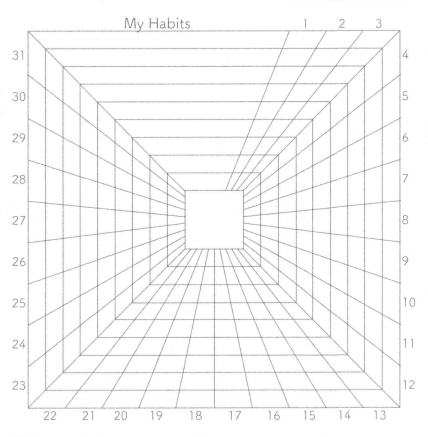

My Habits

31 · 1 2 3 4 5 6 7 8 9 10 11 12 · 23 · 22 21 20 19 18 17 16 15 14 13

Did something go wrong & my response to it:

_____

_____

Something to make next month better:

_____

_____

How I feel about my habits this month:

Month #3

Choose your monthly goals and determine your habits:

Goal(s)

Habit | Trigger / Time

"Good habits are worth being
fanatical about."

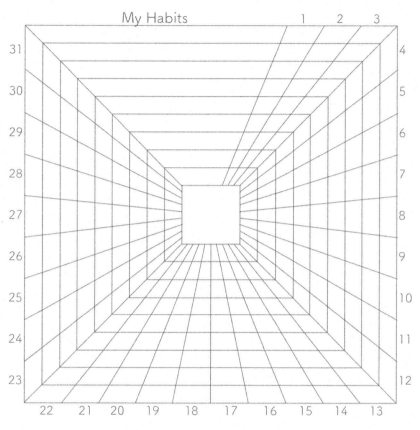

My Habits

Did something go wrong & my response to it:

_____

_____

Something to make next month better:

_____

_____

How I feel about my habits this month:

Month #4

Choose your monthly goals and determine your habits:

Goal(s)

Habit | **Trigger / Time**

"You'll never change your life until you change
something you do daily."

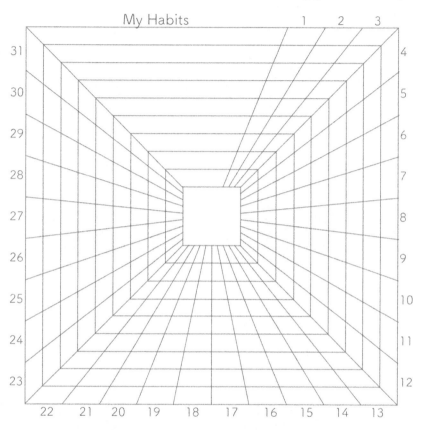

My Habits

Did something go wrong & my response to it:

_____

_____

Something to make next month better:

_____

_____

How I feel about my habits this month:

Month #5

Choose your monthly goals and determine your habits:

Goal(s)

Habit — Trigger / Time

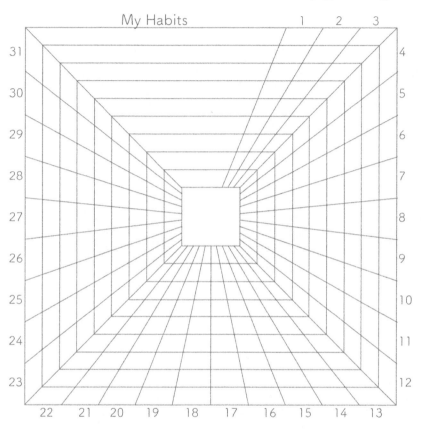

My Habits

Did something go wrong & my response to it:

_____

_____

Something to make next month better:

_____

_____

How I feel about my habits this month:

Month #6

Choose your monthly goals and determine your habits:

Goal(s)

Habit

Trigger / Time

"If 'Plan A' didn't work, the alphabet has 25 more letters. Keep going!"

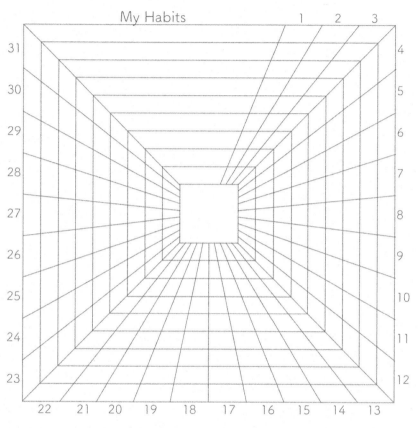

My Habits

Did something go wrong & my response to it:

_____

_____

Something to make next month better:

_____

_____

How I feel about my habits this month:

Month #7

Choose your monthly goals and determine your habits:

Goal(s)

Habit | Trigger / Time

"It does not matter how slowly you go as long as you do not stop."

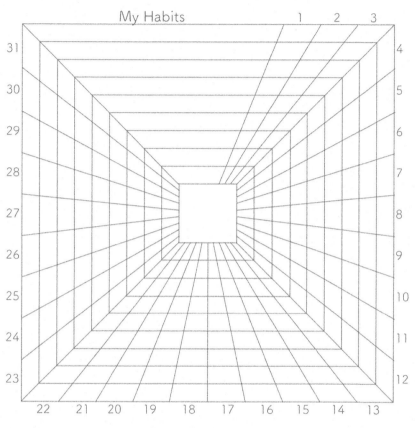

My Habits

Did something go wrong & my response to it:

_____

_____

Something to make next month better:

_____

_____

How I feel about my habits this month:

Month #8

Choose your monthly goals and determine your habits:

Goal(s)

Habit | Trigger / Time

"Failure isn't fatal, but failure to change might be."

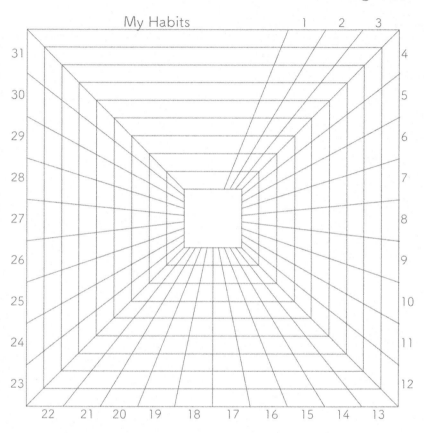

My Habits

Did something go wrong & my response to it:

_____

_____

Something to make next month better:

_____

_____

How I feel about my habits this month:

Month #9

Choose your monthly goals and determine your habits:

Goal(s)

Habit — Trigger / Time

"If you really look closely, most overnight successes took a long time."

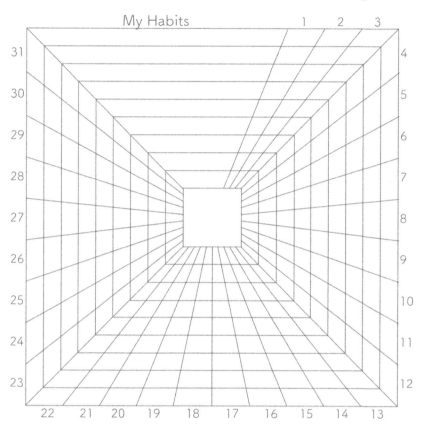

My Habits

Did something go wrong & my response to it:

_____

_____

Something to make next month better:

_____

_____

How I feel about my habits this month:

Month #10

Choose your monthly goals and determine your habits:

Goal(s)

Habit

Trigger / Time

"The difference between who you are and who you want to be is what you do."

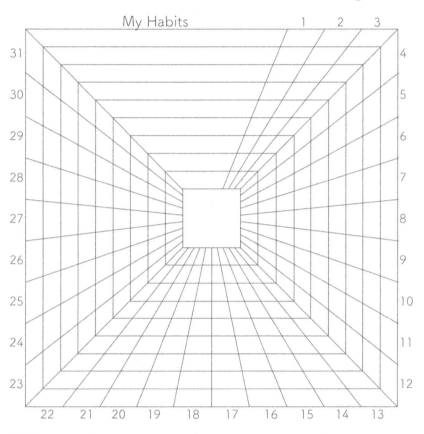

My Habits

Did something go wrong & my response to it:

_____

_____

Something to make next month better:

_____

_____

How I feel about my habits this month:

Month #11

Choose your monthly goals and determine your habits:

Goal(s)

Habit | Trigger / Time

"It always seems impossible
until it's done."

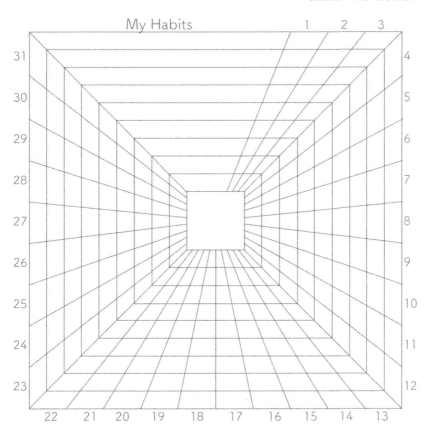

My Habits

31 | 30 | 29 | 28 | 27 | 26 | 25 | 24 | 23

1 | 2 | 3 | 4 | 5 | 6 | 7 | 8 | 9 | 10 | 11 | 12

22 | 21 | 20 | 19 | 18 | 17 | 16 | 15 | 14 | 13

Did something go wrong & my response to it:

Something to make next month better:

How I feel about my habits this month:

Month #12

Choose your monthly goals and determine your habits:

Goal(s)

Habit | **Trigger / Time**

"Success is not final; failure is not fatal: It is the courage to continue that counts."

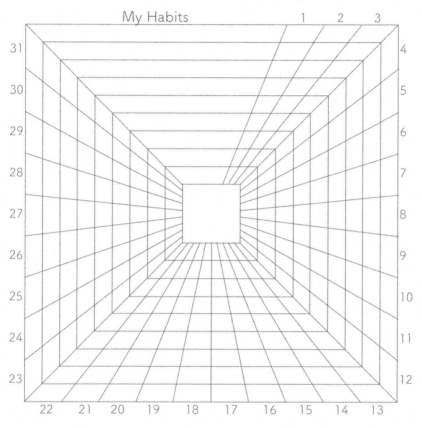

My Habits

Did something go wrong & my response to it:

_____

_____

Something to make next month better:

_____

_____

How I feel about my habits this month:

HAPPINESS LOOKS GORGEOUS ON YOU.
THINK HAPPY, STAY HAPPY!
THIS IS THE ULTIMATE GOAL.

My thoughts...

/ my thoughts /

Hey!

The book you have in your hands is brought to you by Happy Books Hub.
We have a passion for creating books that can improve and add joy to people's lives. Hopefully this journal will accomplish just that for you!

If you have any suggestions on how to improve it, or what we can change or add to make it more useful particularly to you, please don't hesitate to contact us at
hello@happybookshub.com
We would be more than happy to consider how to apply your suggestion to this journal's next edition.

Thank you for buying My 66-Day Habit Challenge journal!

Did you enjoy it?
Please, support us and leave a review!

Love,
Happy Books Hub

Made in the USA
Middletown, DE
02 December 2020

26077602R00040